A tale of self love & self healing

A tale, *YOU decide*

YOU

SAMAR BAKHTAWAR

Acknowledgment

I would like to extend my gratitude to my parents and my sister for always encouraging me and standing by me.
My mother who taught me how to stay strong always and radiate positivity. My father who always made us understand the chemistry of life.
My friends, both the ones who gave up and leave, and the one's that decided to stay; thank you, thank you so much! You all are the reason I am wiser, braver and stronger than ever.
The person who made me believe in myself , stood by me , decided to stay, see me grow and overcome everything I thought I would never be able to move on from ,the list is long and words might fall short but ; this one is for you. This would have never been possible without your support, love and trust in me; عشق من thank you.

Dedication

For my beloved aunt, Dr. Mahmooda Soni Wali (Late) & to anyone trying to recover from things they don't talk about. This is for you. Heal yourself, love yourself.

Life comes with its ups and downs. I pray you are strong enough to stand firm throughout these storms. By the time you realize that life is actually a ride, you either take it or later on regret it. I believe, you will take it, learn from it and bring out the best in YOURSELF.

When you give out the best of your to everyone who crosses your path, I want you to know that the best will come back to you. Consider this as the law of universe; what you give will come back twice of how much you gave.

I pray you give happiness, love, kindness and good manners. In a time where all these things are rare, I pray your heart is always full of these. May your heart always be the softest.

While reading this, know that I unlike you, went through everything you are going through right now and I know it feels like the grey skies will forever be here. Let me tell you a little secret, one fine morning you will have all the courage to heal yourself like no other and that day, you will be stronger than ever. I healed myself and these written fragments are exactly what I did to recover from everything.

May the sun in you shine enough to help you find YOU.

(Ameen)

...to the teenagers and people still stuck in their teenage.

My life is nothing more than

An empty hallway,

A corridor with masterpieces

Hanging all the way down.

"Happiness is around you, embrace it"

You won't find happiness around if it's not within you. Happiness is to be found inside you first and ultimately every little thing will seem to be the source of happiness.

It always starts with you, you have to let go any negative thought that crosses your mind. Your weight age of happiness should always be heavier than that of sadness.

Happy days & sad days, both come together and life happens. You cannot expect things to go smooth always. Once you are contented with even the tiniest things, your day and your life will be filled of a magic called happiness.

You are always one step away from a
totally different life. You decide.
Being happy is a choice.

"Everything will make sense"

Do not lose hope. I know it gets difficult when you are surrounded by negativity and the waiting period keeps getting long. Put your trust, your faith in God. Surely, after a long and tiring journey, the road of patience will end and you will be given the best that you haven't even thought of. You will be given the fruit of your patience and all your hardships, patience, wait, tears and heartbreaks, each and everything will make sense. Believe.

"Rooms where love and kindness speak"

Leave the tables that no longer serve you positive energy. You belong to rooms where love and kindness speak louder than anything else; you belong to places where you and your opinion is respected. You belong to people whose circle of doubt is never around your pure intentions and kind-heartedness for them. You deserve the best and best comes in when you let go of anything that drains you.

"You are your savior"

We all need someone, something to hold on to. We all need someone to lighten our paths somewhere. When you find that someone, welcome them but when they leave make sure you are capable enough of gathering your own shattered pieces. At the end of the day, be that someone you need for yourself.

"...the art of letting go"

Learn to let go.

Sometimes you are stopping the blessings by not letting go the toxicity but the day you let go, all the blessings embrace you like no other.

Let go the anger you hold in yourself, don't suppress your emotions, let go of the idea that keeping your emotions to yourself is the definition of strong. It is not. The day you let go of the anger, your life will get a lot easier. You will find yourself moving in a positive direction.

Forgive people, ask forgiveness. Forgiveness will bless you eventually in ways you never would have thought of, it will open ways that have been closed for so long. It's a two way process, when you don't forgive or don't ask forgiveness, you creates a barrier between you and your beautiful blessings.

Your heart, your soul doesn't deserve any kind of bitterness. Live life to its fullest by letting go of things that poison you.

"...understanding and communication; two ways many things would never mess up"

Understanding someone else's situation the way you want yours to be understood is what makes you stand out from the crowd.

When someone doesn't treat you good, the problem is not with you instead, it's the person in them they are fighting with.
See the bigger picture. Try to understand, try to communicate and make them talk to you so they don't be harsh to themselves either. It might be difficult but understanding and communication; two ways many things would never mess up.

The same thing goes to you too; don't be quick enough to jump to conclusions and cutting off. If someone wants to help you, let them help you.

Life doesn't give you good people twice.
May you always be the one to make
someone's life better to live.

"...a heart that needs to be saved from every bad."

Take care of the beautiful heart you own. The heart that sees the good in people, the heart that hurts when someone else's heart hurts. Heart like yours is rare and indeed what the world needs most right now, heart that forgives, heart that sees the flaws in people yet still holds on when they hate themselves. A heart like yours is a heart that needs to be saved from every bad. You are the reason people believe in the good.

"... do not hold grudges "

When someone does bad to you, do not hold grudges against them and neither hate them. Some people are meant to cross your path in order to make you learn some lessons. Appreciate their temporary presence in your life since they will make you experience things you will get to learn nowhere else.

"...that's how you learn"

Everything that's happened has
happened for a reason. Certain things
happen in order to shape you in whom
you are today, to make you learn lessons
that help you grow.
There's no richer feeling than knowing
that you have became better than who
you were yesterday and shall continue to
be even better for all tomorrows.
Mistakes are made, trust is broken,
hearts are damaged but what matters is
how you change yourself for better. You
need to go through all this, that's how
you learn.
You must be better in your own eyes first
and the people around, later.
You learn from the bad days more than
the good days.

"...save someone's heart today, someone might save yours tomorrow."

Words put a really strong impact on people they are said to. Have a good taste in choosing and saying words because sometimes intentionally or unintentionally we hurt people with the same words that are just words to us but bricks and stones to those whom they are being said. Our words have the power to heal someone, change someone's perspective about everything, mend someone's broken heart, relieve a heart from what they have been caged themselves in or even encourage them for something they have been discouraged for on & off. In a world full of negativity, harsh attitudes and behaviors, be someone with a good taste in words. A good taste in words is far way better than a good taste in clothes and shoes.

There are a lot of people to demotivate
and discourage others. There are people
who get dragged down by these
negativities real quick. Save someone's
heart today, someone might save yours
tomorrow.

"...be a warrior."

The day is near where you will be settled, happy and at peace in life. The day when all the hardships that you went through will make sense. You will look at yourself and smile at how you fought and stood strong against all the difficulties you were put through. They might, at that time, seemed tough but you were put in them for your own good, to be who you are today, to be so unapologetically strong. For now, be a warrior and fight these battles that would only make you win.

"...a fight worth fighting."

Stay strong for yourself. Sometimes you have to fight for yourself. Know that you are a good person, a good friend, and more over a beautiful soul. Relation/friendships that are meant to be, will end up good and which don't, won't end up good. They demand to be fought for but sometimes you have to realize that one person cannot fight the whole time. You have to stop when the other side doesn't give the same energy. People realize the worth of good after losing it. Be good till you can, fight until you can and then be fought for. Let people fight for you after you have done your part. Let people see the good in how gracefully you deal anything life puts you in. You are worth fighting for, you are the person they would go till the end if they are the real ones."

"...make yourself, your heart proud."

You are going to be okay soon. Things are going to be good soon. Good days are coming. Just don't give up. Giving up won't help, it won't sort things out. Remind yourself of how things worse than today have happened, times when you felt the same level of pain, times when you were falling apart, times where you thought there will be no morning to the hurting night.

Remind yourself of how you survived all those days and nights you thought you won't be able to but still made it through. Life has been harsh to you but you still survived and this tells how strong you are as a person.
Breathe and trust that you will survive everything. To struggle is the part of the process

I repeat good days are around the corner. Your patience, your struggles will make sense. Just keep going and know that as long as you don't give up and keep moving forward, no matter how much things seem difficult and tough, you are going to make it and thank yourself for not giving up.

Make yourself, your heart proud.

"...there's always a good side of all the hurt that you go through."

There comes a point in life where you have to leave what you have been wishing on for so long. If it's for you, it won't ever go to someone else and if it's not for you, it won't ever be for you. You have to let go something sometimes for the sake of your own peace of mind. Whether it is someone you love or a thing you want.

When you are kept away from something, you are in other way redirected to something which is beautiful for you in every way.

You are not supposed to let anything disturb you till the point it makes you cut off from everything and everyone.

It will be hard first but eventually your heart will heal and you will understand that there's always a good side of all the hurt that you go through.

"...the strong ones are the kindest, never bitter."

There comes a time in our lives where we get used to the hardships. Some people in return to those hardships get stronger along with their faith that things will take time but shall get easier and go with the flow but some people decide to stay stuck in their current situation and blame every other person for the condition they have been put in. Life doesn't stop, neither in the moments one is happy nor when the person is going through something. It goes on like the flow of water, only moving forward. The strong one isn't someone who goes on faking his strength but someone who stands against all the hardships and hopes for the better that is yet to come. The strong one's are the kindest, never bitter. Never.

The decision is yours. Be careful with what you decide to do so you don't regret it in near future.

"...the people we love stay with us."

When people leave us, they leave a major part of them that resides within us for a very long time. Sometimes, for years and sometimes until the day we give up on life. They stay alive in our hearts. The people we love stay with us, Always.

~a fragment I wrote in 2017, a year after I lost my aunt.

"...you will stumble and fall"

Life will fail you many times just for you to win the battles you don't even know, exist.
You will stumble and fall many times. The bruises don't matter as long as you know how and which backup plan you have to use. God never closes a door without opening another and neither does life feed you; you have to work for things, fight for your rights. Go find the door and get in where you have always wanted to be. God will lighten up your path. God will help you.

"...welcome beautiful beginnings."

Years from now, everything you are worried about today won't matter. People who love you or who you love that aren't healthy for you, you will lose eventually or they will lose you but shall be replaced with who is the best for you. The situations you are facing today will make you strong, fearless and capable of dealing with every situation courageously. The things you are crying about today will make you realize that every tear was worth it. You are going to nod and smile at how foolish you were to cry on things that were supposed to be removed only by replacing it with positivity. Letting go is not easy at all but it's time to let go of that toxicity that is stopping you from becoming better; with a big and an open heart. Let go and that

is how you will welcome beautiful
beginnings.

"...the world works like this"

You know that in this world you are
going to be tested but still you complain
when something bad happens or when
you go through a devastating situation.
Whenever you complain about
something little, remember that
something big and worse than it could
have happened. You have to go through
it. Remember, The world is designed this
way , it works like this.

We are worthy of everything good. We deserve all the love that we give. Repeat this to yourself every time. I know we sometimes think we are not enough but that's exactly when we are. We sometimes end up saying we are worthless, leave no impact on others. You might not be the moon in someone's sky but you are sure that one star they sleep looking at. You may not be the excellent headline one reads over and over again but at the end of the day, your one sentence might be something they sleep believing in. I have been an addict of crime stories so far and one thing I have learned is that •WE LEAVE OUR FINGERPRINTS EVERYWHERE• When you open the doors to positivity, you leave your fingerprints on the handle. Whoever opens the door gets a flashback

to what made you open this door. Your
one word can change someone,
sometimes in the best possible way.

"...do not give up."

Do not give up just because your hard-work doesn't seem like paying off or you are tired of trying to get over something. Things take time and require patience. Take the risks, do your thing, that how you learn and that how you find light.

Right before you give up, ask yourself is this why you came so far, just to give up?

You are stronger than anyone has ever told you. Everything takes time, patience and consistency.

The light is soon to be seen, the results to your hard work are soon to disclose.

***"...you are wiser and stronger than yesterday."**

There are nights, I know, when you are not able to sleep, the heartaches and regrets that hit you in the midst of nights and times where you hate yourself but there's something I realized late but I guess the delay is worth it all and it's that your past is now gone, you can no longer go back or bring changes in it. You have come a very long way and today is all that you have got.

I know it hurts when people who know every page of your life and even know that you are not what you were before , leave like if they were always waiting for a chance to make your past an excuse to leave. Stay away from such people for once and all.

You are not what you were yesterday, you are much better than that, wiser and

stronger than yesterday and people who
are just with you on your good days
don't deserve to see you on your most
wonderful days.

"...re-introduce yourself"

Forgiving is the step on the staircase that leads to healing. You have to forgive yourself for the mistakes you made or for the things you blame yourself for till date. It takes a lot of courage to let go and forgive but that shows how strong you can be as a person.

It's okay, if you won't make mistakes you won't ever be able to know what to not do in the future. Mistakes are a part of life and nothing helps a person in growth more than the mistakes made, trust me.

Your younger self was too young to know what was right and what you were not supposed to do.

I ask you to forgive not only yourself but the people you have crossed paths with. They are gone and so has the younger you. Change for better today , re-introduce yourself.

"...the good things, they always find a way back to the giver."

Never stop being the good person, the kindest.

I know it hurts when in return to your kindness, all you get back is unkind attitudes. I totally understand the hurt that is caused when all you want is good for someone but they just keep neglecting you and your intentions.

Don't stop being the one always being kind, I am repeating this because I have good news for you which is that the kindness you give, the love you give, the selflessness you show will all come back to you. None of the good goes to waste, it always comes back. The good things , they always find a way back to the giver.

It might take a while but it will come back and you will forget all the days you cursed yourself for being too good. I promise.

" ...the art of acceptance."

I used to wonder how do people get over the sad days or how do they move on from bitter memories until this one day when I found the answer.

Acceptance–accepting what happened, accepting that what happened was meant to happen to shape you, to mold you in a better person. Accepting the fact that people who are meant to leave will eventually leave and those who are meant to stay shall stay.

Acceptance is the first step of healing. You cannot expect yourself to heal if you just sit and grief over your mistakes or the people who left or whatever happened in your life.
You have to accept that certain things have to happen in life in order for us to know, in order for us to grow.

Once you start to accept things as they are, life gets a lot easier. Once you start to let things flow, they flow in the best of

directions and take you exactly where
you are to go.

Accept yourself as you are and I promise
you, you will find a list of things to love
about yourself, to change about yourself
and to be proud of yourself.

"...a beautiful ending waits."

If people's way of treating you is totally opposite and hurtful to how you treat them, just know that you are so beautiful at your heart and that regardless of getting hurt, you still wish them good, stand by them and forgive them when they don't ask you a single apology.

I know it hurts but trust me your patience, tolerance; good behavior will not go wasted. Just never give up. It's usually that we are near to the last step when we give up.
You came this far for a reason, don't miss it.

A beautiful ending waits.

"...the state of being strong."

Many people confuse the state of being strong. Being strong in any way doesn't mean to hide your emotions or the pain anything or anyone caused you. It means that you are mentally so indestructible and you have the power to keep going. This is what the word *"strong"* actually means.

Don't confuse being stoned and being strong. Strong people are always emotionally available.

I hope the battles make you strong enough to fight for yourself and the pain makes you realize how important being kind is and to me, the strongest is the one who stays kind and soft-hearted even when the world is against him.

"...to be patient."

I, unlike you, was always told to be patient no matter what. Even if people hurt me to the core. This used to disturb me but in my late-teenage I understood why it was important to be patient.

Today when I look back, I see how being patient was actually making ways for me when I least expected. Being patient will eventually make you see that all the hurt , heartbreak, pain, tears ,everything will make perfect sense.

It's okay to feel lost right now, because that how you will have an urge to find yourself!
Believe in yourself.

" *...bloom like a flower* "

One day you will look back and know that you just got better. All the times you thought life was putting you in tests; it was actually making you strong and fierce. It was making you bloom and you *bloomed* like the flowers do after autumn passes by and spring comes.

"...be kind to yourself."

Progress is slow but the result is always so fruitful. You might not be good at something right now but with believe in yourself and to keep trying will fix everything.

Self love doesn't happen overnight, neither does healing happen overnight. Things take time and patience. Don't you give up! Your wounds need to be treated with love and affection, treat them that way. Your soul needs a time to be understood, make time for yourself.

You are not weak, not at all. You are just being impatient with yourself. Be kind to yourself.

"...the courage to let go."

There will come a time when you will outgrow the people you never imagined living without. This time ,this specific phase of your life will teach you a lot of things and one of them will be letting go when its only you who's putting in all the efforts to save or keep the bond going.

I appreciate you if you have always tried your best to save something but sometimes ,you have to let things go and know that nothing works if 1 out of 2 is giving their all and the other one doesn't even value and appreciate. It will hurt you for a while but once you are emotionally stable, you will stand tall and proud of having the courage to let go something only you were holding on to.

You choose your vibe. Believe me when I say that you decide how you are going to live and which vibe you are going to attract. Don't ever let anyone get comfortable disrespecting you. Let them call you selfish if you are just prioritizing yourself and asking for the respect you unlike everyone deserve.
The right ones ; you won't ever have to doubt their vibe ,they will always understand you even if you take a break from everything and ghost while the other ones would just go around shaming you for asking a self-time.

"...frights and terrors"

I know the heartache you hold from things you still haven't overcome, the fears that still haunt you in the middle of night but you are braver than your frights and terrors, you are stronger than the who you were before. I promise you, these fears are just to let go and not to carry along. You deserve so much good than they say you do.

"…wiser than before"

Untangle yourself from your past. It is gone; you can no longer bring any change in it. You are not even who you were back then. Today, decide to look back not to get yourself hurt but to see how far you've come and how strong and wiser you have become. Stay proud of yourself!

"...the grey skies will leave."

The storm that is raging in you will pass but I hope you know that only you can make peace with it. You have to let it all out and then let it go. The grey skies will leave and beautiful skies shall be seen.

"...all the good will reciprocate"

When going through tough times, I hope you know how worthy you are and how many beautiful things are waiting for you at the end. I hope you know that the love, care and the goodness you give to others, my dear, shall be reciprocated and you will be contented with how alluring the rainbow is after the storm.

" ...re-define yourself."

Your past doesn't define you. You have
moved on from it long ago.
What defines you is how you are going
to make your present beautiful and a
future, even better and beautiful for
yourself. Your mistakes don't define you
but your capability to overcome those
mistakes. What you are today is all that
matters.

May you choose to be full of love and
kindness today.
May you choose to be a positive and
inspiring person.

Life becomes easier when you start
accepting things Instead of spoiling your
today crying over yesterday.

"... you chase what you perceive."

Your mindset is on what your whole life depends.
A positive mindset would result in a happy and positive life where a negative mindset would always keep you disturbed and assume things that might never happen.

You have to find joy in the smallest of things and keep a healthy perspective about everything.

When you chase all the good and positive things, you start to develop a mindset that makes you indestructible.

Your positive mindset would allow positive people surround you and ultimately happiness would surround you.

"... Choose wisely"

Your happiness is in your own hands. You control how your day and life is going to be. Every morning when you wake up, you decide how you are going to spend your day. Choose happiness, choose positivity, choose kindness and choose words that not only help you move in life but people around you too. Choose wisely.

Nobody and nothing can make you happy if you are not ready to let go the negative thoughts and energy that consumes your mind and soul. Your happiness is your responsibility.
Spend your time wisely and with people who add in your mind, positively.

"...time doesn't heal; a myth."

Time does heal if you let it to.
There's nothing that's Impossible. It's us,
we have made things complicated. Time
and patience make everything easy. You
just need to let things happen on their
own specific time. The harsh memories
you want to get over require time. There
comes a time when you are blessed with
so much happiness and joy that you
forget what hurt you in the past. Time
changes and so does situations. People
who were so dear to you and left
somehow, the hurt of their departure
will eventually go away only it you
accept that whatever happened had to
happen.

It's all about how you handle things.
It's all about how you treat yourself and
people around you while healing from
things that hurt you.

"... life - a maze."

When life puts you through tests, know that you are worthy and valuable. Just because you are on your bad days doesn't mean your whole life is bad.

You need to repeat to yourself how brave you are actually.

Good days and bad days happen to everyone, how you tackle and find the good in the bad makes you stronger than ever.

Life's a maze and In order to find the way out , to find light , you need to go In every direction and go through everything that makes you brave enough to fight and stand for yourself and help others when they are going through something you went through

"... Help them get through something they are struggling with."

When someone tries to help you, advice you for your own good and love you regardless, I hope you know what you are supposed to do.
I want you to be the person they trust afterwards, I want you to be someone they get happy helping.

In a world like today, people no longer entertain kindness and generosity whereas being kind and generous to others should be as important as anything.

It takes few words to make someone's day better and to help them get through something they are struggling with.

Compliment people. Appreciate the smallest efforts someone makes. Respect the feelings someone shows you, you don't know how much courage they must have gathered In order to share their feelings with you. Talk In such a tone that the other person feels comfortable sharing and talking with you.

***"... a taste of their own medicine."**

You don't have to give them a taste of their own medicine to let them know how poorly they are treating you. Instead, be kind.

Treat them with love; treat them in such a great manner that they understand how they should treat themselves and others too.

People who are hurt often hurt others. Such people need healing and fixing the most and are not strong enough. For such people, I pray you become the person who helps them and fix them, make them fall in love with themselves and forget the harshness they have faced.

Mistreating them just because they mistreated you is immature. Whenever you get mistreated, promise yourself that you will never make anyone feel the way someone else made you feel. That's what makes you a human.

Do not give up and neither gets tired of
always being the strong one, that's your
power.

May you know it.
May you be proud of it

"... a break from life."

You are allowed to switch off your phone. You are allowed to deactivate your social media handles and take a break from life. Don't get easily influenced of whatever you see, sees the bigger picture, try to look behind the curtains. Life is not perfect at all; we make it perfect for us by keeping a mindset that's nothing but beautifully positive.

Take a break from everything that disturbs your peace of mind. If you want to take a break from the relationships you hold with yourself then always know that you don't have to fear then leaving, the right ones stay no matter what. They are mature and understanding enough to help you get through all and stand with you through everything. Appreciate them, don't forget to value them and hold them close.

"...a tale of self love and self healing."

Love yourself before you love anyone else and want to be loved, respect yourself before anyone else respects you. Take care of your heart before you want it to be taken care of. Heal yourself before your heal anyone else. Accept yourself with all your flaws and Imperfections and you shall be able to accept others and be accepted

Self love and self healing will make you happy and strong. Your life should be a tale of self love and self healing.

Once you are healed and you love yourself, threes nothing that can break you. There's nothing that you can't do and there's absolutely no-one that you can't heal and make them fall in love with them.

"… sometimes the best you can do is sit back and relax."

Stop over thinking.
Life is not supposed to give you a
solution to every situation.
Know that everything happens in exactly
the same way it's supposed to happen. It
always does. You need to trust the
timings and your gut. Sometimes you
don't know what to do and what to not
and that's okay. Sometimes the best you
can do is sit back and relax.

"... a heart that works."

Most of the times, I was told that I am "too sensitive" and I should work on myself. People made me believe that there's something wrong with me and feeling things too deeply , being "too kind " Is something I should change about myself. I started to work on my sensitivity and pretended that certain things don't touch me anymore.

Apologised for every-time my eyes watered and stopped sharing my heart out until this one day that I realised there was nothing wrong with me and most of all nothing wrong with a heart that feels, cares, loves and worries for others

" ...a promise that is sometimes not kept."

The fact is that the more people get to know about something or someone, the more clear things become and that is why most of the relationships fail. Whether friendships or any bond.

People are too quick to say that "we will accept anyone with their flaws, mistakes and their past" but when the time comes, they back off. They decide to leave and make the other person hate them-self to such an extent that they stop opening up to anyone and that's the worst thing that can happen.

Be kind to people. Accept them with whatever people have to serve. It takes a lot of strength to open up to anyone. Respect their strength.

I pray people mean whenever they say, they will stand by you and not leave you when grey clouds cover up your sky.

"...make peace with yourself."

You need to be at peace with your mind and soul and with the closest people. You cannot expect a hopeful and peaceful future if you are not at peace with your past.

You cannot be at peace with your surrounding if you are not at peace with yourself. Peace comes within. The peace in your soul reflects in your thoughts and ideas.

You have a heart to motivate you. Let it motivate you to an extent that you are happy and contented with yourself before anyone else.

Everyone has a past. Things they are afraid to share loud. It's okay, as I said everyone has one. Some let it go while some think upon it a bit too much.

I have seen people who belittle the other after knowing their past or the mistakes they have made and also repeat same things to them which are quite disturbing and adversely affect one's mental health.

People still need to learn a lot of things and one of them is to learn that an individual musters up a lot of courage to open up about something that has hurt them in the past. Respect that.

Learn about someone's past or grief not to further disrespect or devalue them but to help them stand up straight and heal.

Some people out here just need someone to listen to them. If you can be nothing,

be a good listener because someday
someone might listen to you when you
need it the most.

"...you are the sun in their lives, they will come back to you when it gets dark."
It's okay if your favorite person never puts you first or the people you would risk it all, always put you second. It's totally okay.

I know your heart that hurts every time you hear something or see someone putting you second when in all your time spent with them you have kept them first. You have considered them your *go to* person on good as well as bad days.

You didn't ever put them second even when they made you feel worthless and all the nights you went to the bed feeling unworthy because of them.
I know it hurts but, have you ever looked at the other side? At the end, they always come back to you no matter what.
I know till then the hurt has actually hurt you a lot but that's where you learn that not everyone has a heart like yours.

Never be harsh towards them , always
stay kind because one day , when they sit
alone and take out time to list the people
who were always there but they couldn't
see because of all the people they kept
before you , I hope you believe me when
I say this that they will only write your
name. Your name as the person they
threw so much harsh behavior at, so
much coldness at. The person who stayed
and never made them feel how they
made you feel.

You are the sun in their lives, they will
come back to you when its gets dark.

Have patience. People often realize late
but they do.

Don't stop being kind.

"...open your eyes to the blessings in disguise."

Life happens to everyone. For some it's losing loved ones while for others it's struggling with several other things.

While life happens, we get tired and hurt and the pain often leads to severe breakdowns but I guess without pain, we would have never been able to know how it feels to experience happiness and joy after all the struggles.

Certain thing has to happen for us to be grateful and see a broader view.

Without heartbreak, one might never be able to know the meaning of how it feels to be truly loved and adored. Without refusals, one might never know the joy that surrounds when one experiences acceptance. Without negative people around, one might never be able to appreciate the positive people.

The pains that you question, the situations that you question have led you till here to know that this is life and it all depends on how you take the situation and make use of it. Either you sit back and cry or you get up and see what actually lies behind.

Grow through these. Trust me when I say that life is full of challenges, challenges that are for you to take.

These challenges and hard times will make you wiser and stronger only if you keep going and not give up.

Find your purpose in these hard times and pain. The best life, the great life you want to live cannot be lived without challenging situations.

Be the person who sees purpose and blessings in pain.

***"...life is too short to stay in the past."**

Some people grow up physically but emotionally, they're stuck in their teenage which at times adversely affects their present., they decide to live with the rough teenage they lived through and wish to let it stay with them instead of letting it go and that is why such people experience an unstable present.

The person they were before when they lost someone precious or got mistreated never gets to fix itself.

You will know such people by the way they would treat you, hesitate in opening up to you, might not even be mentally matured to communicate over several topics and maybe push you away when you try to help them.

Stick through them. They are the ones that need you the most and you are the one they need to get rid of the grief that makes them so harsh and cold.

They will be rude towards you at times; they might even push you away. Be kind, they need support and recovery. Make them trust your intentions, let them know you love them and you care for them and that you want nothing but good for them.

Such people have never tried to help themselves and when someone comes along to understand them, help them and advice them for their better, they become resistant and stubborn. They doubt every good thing. All these years, everyone has agreed with all their moves and none of them tried to pour in some good advice and so few things they have got used to.

Reach out to them and if you are the someone who needs help and wants to get rid of the grief that has become anger and coldness, reach out to the one who cares for you. Life is too short to stay in the past and punish the present self and people who are with you.

Free yourself from yesterday's bitterness. There's so much happiness and love, embrace it. Life doesn't stop at any point, it goes on.

"... choose love"

Love is not only good days or how someone acts when they are on good terms.
Love is sacrifice. It's accepting someone's flaw and be with them regardless. Love is knowing the darkness of someone yet deciding to jump in and help them find light. Love is careful.

Choose love.

Don't rush. The right person will find you when you least expect someone to join in your life and make It beautiful. To help you outgrow the dark nights and gloomy days.

"... be someone's sunshine."

Whatever you do has a consequence.
Be a good person, serve kindness and
generosity and it shall come back to you
twice of how much you gave.

Make people smile on their bad days
and, so maybe someday someone makes
you smile when you need it the most.

Make people love themselves, so
someday when you need love, they might
fill you with it.

You are a sun, shine bright in skies that
need it the most.

Appreciate people over little things, so
someday someone appreciates you too
for the efforts you make.

FAIRY TALE
IN
FAIRY LAND

Her fight with cancer

I have seen her breathing while fighting
I used to wish, each wasn't her last
In those days, whatever time we got to
share
I didn't want it to end
Her breaths continuously ending,
My heart, breaking
I wasn't ready for any cruel ending
But I, for sure, couldn't deny the ultimate
truth
I couldn't see her last breath go into the
air
But I was, surely, able to feel another
soul in me
For the rest of my life

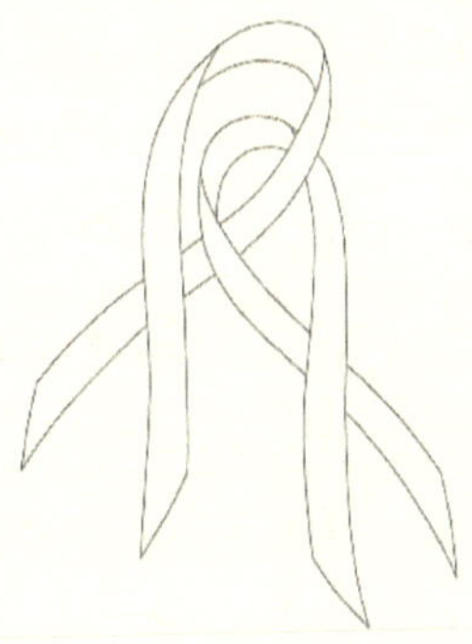

My life; an ocean

My life is like an ocean, so deep
And I, another watercraft
I keep heading to where the waves take
me
The anchor of my past pulls me to the
core of ocean
And I, I stuck into the chain of numerous
sorrows and beautifully broke the heart
Like the cracking wood of the boat
I sink, sink down again
But this time I promise to repair all
The damage to my boat, myself
This time I will move with the anchor
Which carries with it my rough past
And I will make it to the shore
Where once I was a walking sad soul,
tomorrow I will be the person
Ready to fight the storms raging.

I'll be with you

I won't die completely
I will be with you, like the wind
I will mark my existence with the first
ray of sun
In the darkest nights,I will be the stars
you count
And indeed, the moon to light up your
path
Your shadow in the day, your soul in the
night
I will be the kind autumn rain
And the gentle wind touching you
The flake of snow in winters yet the fog
every morning
You will find me everywhere around, I
will be with you
I won't die completely, I won't sleep.

What you think is your weakness is
actually your strength.
Your strength lies in your kindness and
love for others
Your strength is right there in your way
of helping others heal and evolve
Your strength lies exactly in everything
you think is your weakness

You are the reason
I feel alive
On days when it feels so miserable

In the end, it all traces back to a calm
October morning.

In that moment I knew,
You were exactly my heart was longing
for

In those eyes, I found eternity.

I have seen in your eyes
The shade of brown that is so bright.

The kind of brown I always admired
The kind that sparkle when the sun
shines.

And if someday,
Sadness lingers in your eyes
I promise to give you all the happiness.

If someday,
Your paths seem dark
I promise to lighten up with all I have.

If someday,
You ask me to fix you
I promise I will break myself to mend
you.

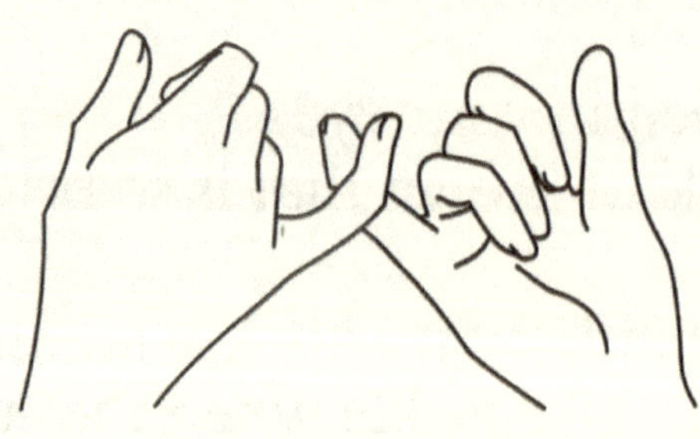

For now, all I have is
You and I
And a colorful sky
Underneath which,
My soul dances to the
Rhythm your heart beats make.

The universe smiles, when you smile.

You are my favorite symphony.

In the middle of night
If I cross your mind,
Listen to your beats
I'd be there for eternity

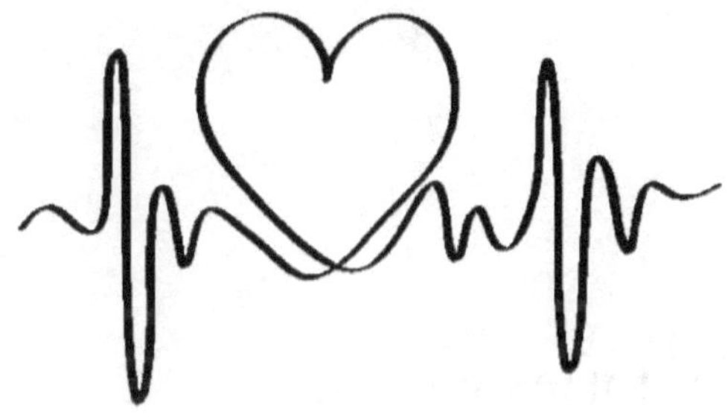

And even in a crowd, my eyes will
always search for you.

Your memories visit me
In all the places we have ever been

The adore, the warmth
I have felt it all

I was asked one day,
To name the bravest person I know
I thought
For a while and replied;
The person who stands by
No matter what
And the one who still speaks
Volumes of kindness
Even after all they get back is hurt

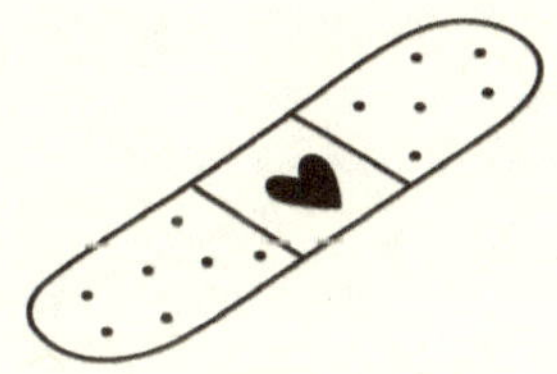

The fire they have
Put you in
I wish you evolve and bloom
Beautifully
Through the ashes

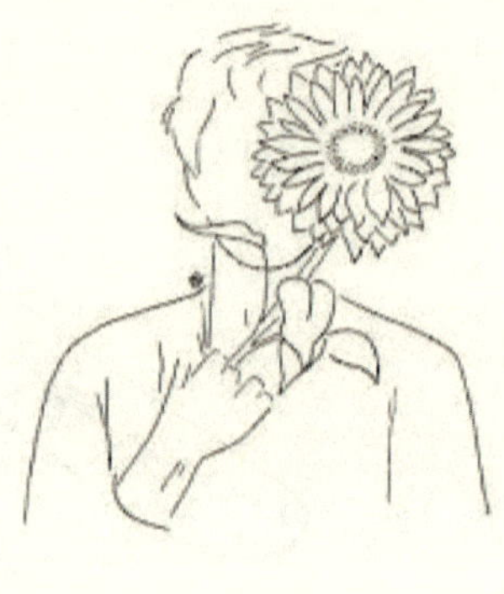

Life

It's when you lay on your couch in the middle of the night and stare at the stars thinking why they shine when there's no one clapping for them.
It's when you stand by your window opposite to the bright sun watching the cloud game.
It's when you feel alone in a room full of people.
It's when you feel appreciated standing in front of the mirror with no one else in the room.
It's when you cry without reasons you feel hurt.
It's when you laugh with the reason you are hurt.
It's when you feel disappointed without keeping any expectations.
It's when you feel overwhelm with keeping expectations.
It's when you feel death without dying and feel life without living

It's a four alphabet story; Life
which requires seven alphabet words;
courage
To live, to stand tall

The storm is
About to pass
And a rainbow
Is to be seen
Have patience
Have faith

Your companionship is my strength
Your love keeps me going
And your support doesn't let me break
down

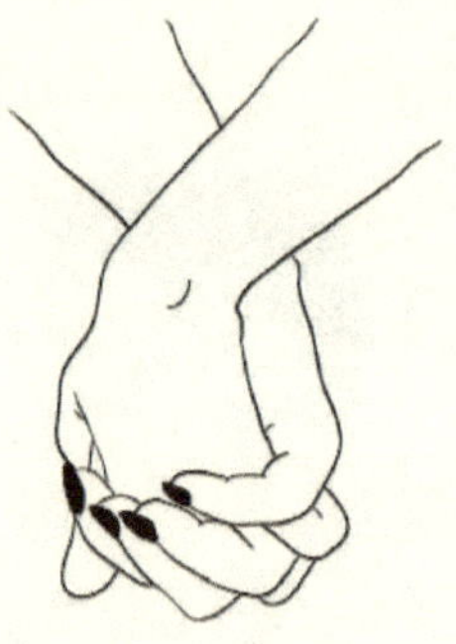

To the lost friends
And to the people I ever knew
I wish you nothing but
Happiness and joy
Sunshine and rainbows
Love and kindness

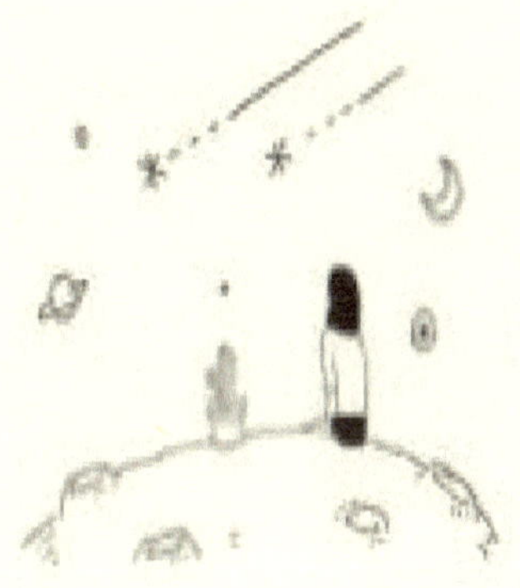

I wonder why you
Call yourself weak
At times
When all I have seen is
You getting stronger
Every time
Something breaks you

The first time I saw you
Across the crowd, I understood
All the times when they said;
Your guts would recognize the one,
The one for you
The eternity you would believe in.

My love grows stronger for you everyday
In your warm embrace, I've promised us
a beautiful forever.

I have talked
To the stars
About you
And
My heart holds
Nothing but you,
close to it.

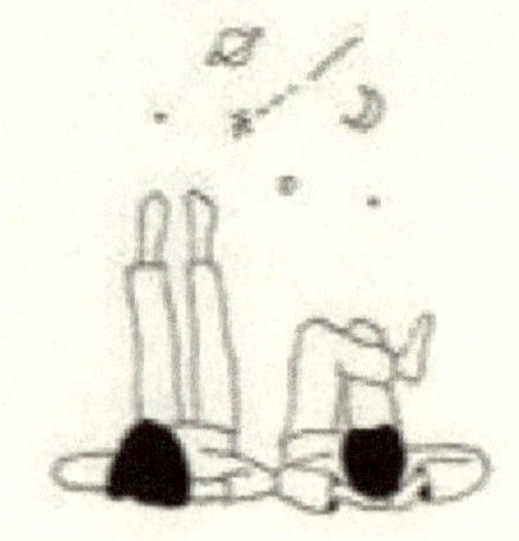

You need to forgive yourself
And love yourself ,
For the mistakes don't define you but
Today you have an opportunity
To define yourself

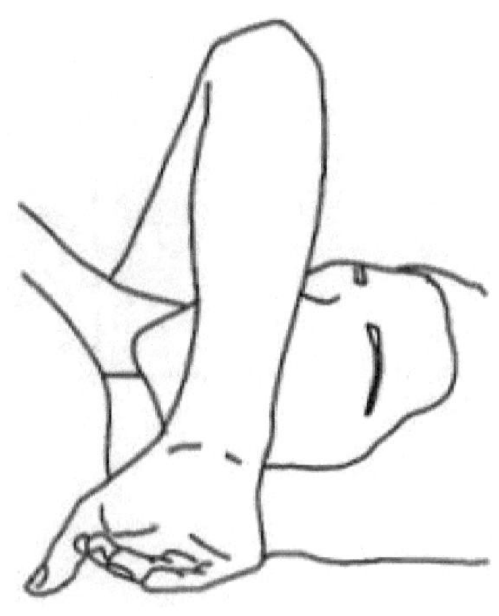

Your memories don't make me sad
anymore
You are in a better place, they say
But, I miss you on my happy days
And your voice still echoes in my mind.

Always appreciate and thank people who
add the element of happiness and hope
in your life and help you love yourself a
bit more than usual and be kind to your
heart.

Don't let your heart ache over things that won't matter after few years.

Some people
Might not be beautiful the way you
define beautiful
But
They for sure, would have a beautiful
heart
You don't ever want to lose.

LETTERS

[A letter to my best friend and the love my heart longed for]

To my best friend;

I found my best friend in you the very first day we met, day when you made me feel the most comfortable. It was when you took care of me when I didn't even know your name but you did.

I found someone who listened to me cry in the middle of night and made me laugh afterwards. In you, I found an ever-lasting friendship and a love, so limitless.

With you, I took baby steps to grow into who I am today. You are the person my heart waited for all these years. You saw me breaking, crying, falling apart yet decided to stay and hold onto me.
Because of you, my heart feels one again.

I found the person I prayed for, in you.

Regards,

The person who will stand by you,
forever.

[Letter to the lost friendships]

Dear lost friend,
                    I knew it happens but
I never wanted it to happen to us.

From talking every day to a complete
silence, how could you let it happen?

I don't claim to be a saint or virtuous but
I am glad and satisfied that I kept trying,
till the end of the line and it was you
who waited every~time to give up on the
friendship and move on.

So when I was done putting in all the
efforts to reconcile and fix , I for once ,
stopped and realized that it was only me
who was trying to save our friendship
from falling apart and that day , I
gathered all the courage to let you go.

It hurts, even though I have moved on
and your voice no longer echoes in my
mind and I don't miss your laugh
anymore. For once, I wished, you could
have fought and let go the reasons for

the sake of our friendship but you decided to choose the reasons instead of us and its okay because you have made me learn so much.

Today, I just want you to know that I am happy and contented, your absence disturbed me for very long but now I have moved on because life is supposed to go on and not stop at one point.

Thank you for the memories you have given me and thank you for the days you made me laugh. I hope where ever you go, happiness goes with you.

Good-bye!

Love,
A friend of yours.

[Letter to the men of our society]

Respected men,
Here's something I wrote
for you.

I hope you know that we appreciate all
the struggles and efforts you do.
I know all the times, since childhood,
you have been told to conceal and
suppress your emotions and your tears.
All the times you got tired of being the
strongest and you wanted to take a break
but you were always seen as someone
whose only job is to be the breadwinner
and hide all the stress and exertion he
feels.

I know all the times when you showed
your damaged heart or spilled out all
your emotions and heard someone say
that you are weak.

This is for you.

You are not weak. Showing your emotions, having watered eyes when something hits your emotions is okay. You don't have to turn your heart into a stone and hide whatever is that you feel and be harsh to yourself. The more you hide your emotions, the harsher you will be to yourself and ultimately your aggressiveness will lead you to be negative and angry. Let that toxicity go. You are a human too. You deserve to speak your heart out too. You like every other person or gender have the right to be vocal about your emotions. Being vocal is not weak, it's strong. Communicate.

You are allowed to take a break and enjoy your life when you are tired of your 9:00 am-5:00pm routine.

You are appreciated. We appreciate you.

Whether you are a man dealing with studies.
Whether you are man dealing with the deadlines your boss has put in front of you.

Whether you are man who is having a hard time managing business / job and home.
Whether you are a husband and father who is unable to enjoy family time.
Whether you are a man who is worried for his future and finding a job.

Relax.
You will get through this all. Do not lose hope. Be vocal. You will radiate happiness and positivity once you set yourself free from everything that you hide.

Regards,
A sister, a daughter, a partner & someone who believes in communication and expressions.

[Letter to the person who tried to take their life once]

Dear person!
I don't know you personally but I know how you tried to harm yourself.

I know you are tired of listening to a voice only you can listen to. I know you are scared of the demons that reside in your mind, the ones that are so loud that you have lost your positive energy.

I know how hard you have tried to hide it all and how difficult it has been lately to keep a smile and pretend like all is well with your heart and mind.

I know that you are completely exhausted fighting a battle only you know about and how scared you are to tell anyone because you fear them judging you and leaving you.

But there's something I want you to know, you are so strong. I appreciate you

for how far you have come, how tired
you have been and still didn't give up.

Do not give up. Trust me.
Stick around. I know I am not standing
in your shoe right now but once I have
stood right where you are today. All
these sleepless nights and painful
thoughts, I know them all.

I ask you to hold on to this pain which
you think has no end but believe me , I
see a beautiful tomorrow that you might
not be able to see right now.
Only if you gather up a little more
strength and know that the pain is about
to end and happiness is all ready to
surround you.

Possibilities and opportunities, happiness
and your dreams are waiting for you if
you only stick around a bit more.

There's people out there life is waiting
for your paths to cross with, people who
have their hearts full of love for you.
Don't give up please.

You are a warrior.
You are the strongest.
I am proud of you for fighting so long,
victory is near.

Regards,
Your fellow warrior.

[Letter to the lost]

Dear lost soul,

   I know right now life feels messed up and you feel lost and I can see you giving up through those eyes that are not shinning like before but I hope you know that you are not alone. Find yourself in this mess. Yes! You read it right, find yourself in this mess.

I hope you find what you were looking for before life hit you.

I believe that everything has a reason and these days where you think like you are lost are actually days where life needs you to figure out things you are capable of yet unaware.

I want you to dig in to your heart and find the passion you and the world needs right now. I hope you know that you are stronger than these thoughts that occupy your mind and convince you to feel weak. I hope you discover the beautiful heart you own and a soul that sparks so bright.

I want you to know that you are unbreakable. I know it feels like everything is falling apart but on days like such, practice the purest form of self love. Remind yourself how appreciable you are and how worthy you are and that it's okay to reach out for love and guidance.

Ask for help, reach out to the person you trust or to anyone you feel like would help you in the best of ways and I guarantee you that there's people out there waiting to help, waiting to listen to you so do not be ashamed of asking help, them and we are here to pick you up when you fall.

I hope you know you are loved and how much compassion you hold within yourself.

Sincerely,
Someone you can talk to.

[Letter to my new friend/s]

Dear friend/s,

When I first talked to you, it was the time when I was completely shattered and numb. I was going through a lot but here's something for you that I couldn't say before.

I used to think the strongest friendships are those that have spent years together, how silly! It sad to see today that the friends I spent many years with couldn't understand me and neither ever tried to the way you did.

You coming in my life are something words might not do justice with but thank you, thank you for joining in and understanding me like no other. You have been motivating me and appreciating me like you always knew me.

Never have I been able to pour everything I feel in words before I became friends with you. I am so glad you are the person I can be myself around and I, without hesitation can share anything I feel. From ranting about my day to crying in voice notes, from arguing to making each other laugh I guess I found the person, the friend/s I can count on.

I know I can trust you with my biggest secrets yet the silliest things I have ever done in life without the fear of being judged.
I love how whenever one of us feels low and the other cheers up and how we equally pour love, care, trust and efforts into this friendship.

I don't know what life has in store for us but I hope life doesn't take you away.

Thank-you for keeping up with my tantrums and sudden breakdowns, for listening to me and staying with me on my worst. Thank you for becoming my beacon of light when I need end it the most. Thank you for staying and choosing my heart and mindset over the fact that I, unlike others, have so many flaws. Friend/s like you is rare.

The next time I see you, I might hug you tighter to let you know that you are an important part of my life and that you matter.

I love you, my best friend.

Love,
Your friend.

[Letter to the person who feels tired of being strong and kind]

Dear!
    I know you feel tired and hurt after being nothing but kind and keeping good intentions even if people threw bricks and stones at you.

This is for you.

The world we reside in, here being harsh, rude and matching someone else's disrespect is really easy. People have made it easy by normalizing it which I know is really wrong. In such a world, my dearest, if you have a control over your mind that continuously tells you to be like them and you continue being *YOU*, you are the strongest.

I know all the nights you have cried asking God to replace your heart with a stone but the next morning you continue being even kinder and stronger because that what you have come so far. You are here for a reason; this is something I strongly believe in.

You are the reason; someone believes that in a world so cruel, goodness still exists. You are the reason; someone might change themselves for better. Who wins? You, my beloved. In the end, the kind people win.

You should be grateful of how you own such a blessed heart.
 A heart that works. A heart that feels the pain when others are in pain. A heart that gets happy when others are happy & a heart that wants to help people.

I am proud of you. Someday, someone will be thankful to you for not giving up on them and for staying kind all the way long and that day you will see how they would want to be like you.

Have patience.

Regards,
Someone who was as tired once as you are.

[Letter to the kids who grew up in an emotionally unstable family]

Hello, can we talk?

I know you are grown up in a very graceful person now but the child in you, ever looked back at him/her?

Don't let that child in you suffocate.

I am sorry if you had a rough childhood and a family that made you grow up having fears and insecurities.

I am sorry if you are afraid to share your secrets because you have faced a life full of mistrusts.

I am sorry if you have struggled with your mental health. I am sorry if you have struggled with your education.

I am so sorry if you grew up learning to let go things that brought you happiness. I am sorry if you lost the shine of your eyes while growing up.

I am sorry if you grew up seeing other families enjoying the best time.

Even today, what you felt as a little kid goes with you everywhere. I know you tried to stay positive and didn't let bitterness take a control over you. I am so proud of you.

This is for you to know that it was not your mistake. Going through everything was for a reason and you are so close to that beautiful reason.

I see you happy, I see you building a happy and peaceful family in near future. I see that potential in you.

I know the hurt you faced as a child is still there, the flashbacks that haunt you even today but look at you, such a kind and strong person.

There's a child in you, tell him/her that life is better now and would keep on getting better.

One day everything is going to make
sense. I promise.

Regards.

[Letter to my younger self]

Dear me,
        You have taught me things in the past,I maybe would have never learned. I am grateful to you today and I will always be. You, on every step, have told me that mistakes are an important part of growing up into the kind of human you wants to be.

Mistakes give you lessons you won't ever find in books or libraries. You will find them in the deepest corners of your soul which will, someday, enlighten the inner and outer you. You taught me that some people are the human form of lessons, once they leave, you understand the real meaning of maturity and growing up. Not only this but that in the process of growing up, some people will leave and some will quit your life, eventually. You just have to understand when to react and when not to.

My dear past, you have taught me many things, things that have made me positive in different ways. Thank you.

Regards,
Present-Me.

[A letter I received from life lately.]

Dear reader,
              I am not always going to be good and positive towards you. I am going to give you so many things you will love passionately but unfortunately,I will take them away when the time ends. I am going to give you a thrilling coaster ride you have a fear of deep within your heart. It will come to an end and I will give you, eventually what you want. I am going to give you hard times and take people away from you. I am going to make you sad for your betterment, so don't blame me, please.

I want you, in the end, to be brave and be a person with a beautiful heart, mind,and soul. I don't want you to give up after all the trials I made you face. What was the purpose of fighting then?

I want you to be forgiving and kind. Hide
your weaknesses and show up your
strong points. I want to see you happy.
I'm sorry for all the hard times.

Regards,
Life.

[Letter to the teenagers and young adults]

This is actually not a letter but a bunch of things that I learnt from the age of 15-19 and keeping in view the lessons and the points I am all set to enter a very sensible, full of challenges stage and a professional age where I will be psychologically developed and shaped and whatever is that I choose would keep a great impact on me and my life. There are few things that I learnt and really wanted to share before I wind up this book and it reaches to you.

We all use social media and I think you won't be unfamiliar with an excerpt that says, "The age of 15-19 is where you lose friends and people you thought you will go very long in life with." You will make mistakes but that's how you learn. We all go through this phase of life, the discovery phase where you discover yourself. You will make mistakes, you will fail but that's how you would know what the right thing to do is and what's not. When you fail, you will have the urge to try again and again till you succeed. When you feel lost, there's a desire you have to find yourself and that's only possible when you have a mindset, a mindset that wants to get educated over things and wants to be a better human. In this phase of life, you will meet people, have emotional attachments and when one day they decide to leave, it will hit you in your emotions and boom! You will try to isolate yourself. Trust me when I say that it will be after a very short span of time that you will be embracing happiness and good vibes, you will finally have people who would stand by you on your worst behavior, help you find yourself and appreciate you and I swear, you won't have to question their genuine care and love for you. You just have to believe that not everyone would do you bad, there are so many good people out there. Don't reject the good that comes to you. Nature has its way of sending help; welcome them with an open heart.

Then comes the young adult age, most of us haven't entered this experimental age but if you are someone who has entered yet having a hard time, this is for you. The age from 20 and onwards is where life starts to put things in their respective places. You get near to graduating university , start a professional life , have an urge to be surrounded by positive energy and most of all it is exactly the time period where if you have matured ,you want to change few toxic things about you and I guess that's the most amazing part. Getting to know your flaws and changing yourself, letting people help you without being offended is the most sensible thing ever. There are many people I know personally that are never stopped from few things or educated over few matters which has made them stubborn and now when someone tries to make them understand , advice them for their own good ,they push them away. There comes a time where if we don't let go of our past , our previous toxic version or things that make our personality toxic , they get firm and no matter how hard someone tries ,it takes very long to change for the GOOD and BETTER !

Since, I will turn 20 really soon and the things I have learnt is sometimes you have to go through few things because they will make you learn so much. It doesn't matter how bad it made you feel, look at what it made you learn and your whole perspective will change towards many things. I came across toxic people who made me grateful for the urge I keep to bring positive change in myself. The cold hearted made me grateful for the soft heart I own. I realized how life was never about fancy things, it was always about the little things and experiences I was scared of doing. Life has been always about taking risks and ending up creating amazing memories. I, somehow concluded that nobody could make me happy and positive unless and until I was ready to let go of the bitterness I hold within myself. In the journey of finding happiness and positivity, being kind and empathic there were days where I used to hate myself because the people I wanted to show up for, let them know that I care about them, the same people pushed me away and made me feel like I have no place in their lives but I knew that these challenges were exactly what I was supposed to go through. I had to be patient with such people and sensitive enough to understand their position and deal them with love and care and so I started to hold them close to myself. I had to give them time to make peace with themselves first but in all this, I realized how beautiful the human heart is that when it loves someone and cares for them, it doesn't give up!

Sometimes in life, you don't need to be a great friend. You just need to be a great human and a kind stranger!

I hope each of you all develop a very positive and happy mindset. I pray you all become the best version of yourself and be able to help someone live life the way it is supposed to be lived.

A reason & some answers

Hello!
So you made it till the end, thank you!
Thank you for joining me in my journey.

Life has been a roller coaster, a ride that
was quite hard but every aspect of it
had something to ponder upon.

Unlike you, I went through the phases
where I had choices to make and
decisions to take and I did make choices,
I did take decisions.

YOU came into existence when life took
some major turns and it was one fine
morning that I decided to sit back and
have a good time with myself and ask
myself a list of *whys* and *what's*. It was
exactly when I knew what I have to do
and YOU happened.

My life made me learn so much that
today when I think of several things, my
mind has matured enough to talk about

them without the fear of being judged or belittled.

Some days are like that where you sit and smile at your past, the same things that once hurt you no longer hurt you today because *YOU* have learnt the art of letting go things you can no longer control and you have come to a conclusion that the very things you thought were hurting you, they were actually making you better. Mistakes are good, that how you learn. So I mustered the art and it led me to happiness and positivity.

From failed friendships I learnt that friendships were never about who stays longer, it was always about who stays when there's one reason to stay and a 100 reasons to leave. It was always about who chooses you over your mistakes. It was who decides to stay and help you correct yourself and heal, not who makes fun of your insecurities.

From failures I learnt that you can never have success after success if you have never failed. I learnt that in order to achieve something, you have to go through trials and you have to struggle.

From poor treatments and attitudes I learnt how kindness was important and how it had a huge impact on others and even your own self. It was exactly when I learnt that self love and self acceptance kept so much importance too. Once you are good to yourself, you automatically are good to others.

I often asked myself the purpose of my being but could never figure out a much satisfactory answer until the day I found out that my words had the power and the least I could do was help someone have a good day and so I did. One after another, those smiles after they talked to me, I started to live for them. I realized that every time someone smiled, the pain in my heart felt a lot less.

In this long run, I realized that life is beautiful and we have messed it up. Life, for sure, comes with tests and trials but never without a way out or solutions.

The day I started realizing these small things was exactly when I started to find myself and luckily, I found myself. Life started to get easy because of the one rule that I started to follow;

"Let go of what you cannot control. All these roughness and toughness is leading you to your destination. A beautiful destination. Be patient."

There came a time where I had to decide between staying kind or go cold and I decided kindness over everything. It hurts sometimes when the kindness goes unnoticed or for granted but there is one thing that is for sure, "kindness will win".

This all didn't happen overnight. It took longer than a while but I am so glad I made it till here and I hope that you will keep going too. It all requires a positive mindset and a heart full of good will and I promise you there's nothing that can stop you from helping yourself and people around you. You will be tested, refused and denied. You might even start

to hate yourself but do not give up. Do
not stop being kind. In the end, you will
see all the reasons that will make you
realize why I stopped you from giving
up.

کہ داستانیں اور بھی ہیں لکھنے کو

مگر اشکوں کی روانی اجازت نہیں دیتی کہنے کو

If at any page, you felt like I am talking
to you then yes I am talking to you and I
guess I have talked to myself too.

I would like to thank all of you once
again. I hope someday, someone amongst
you becomes the reason someone
breathes in life and happiness. I hope
you become the reason someone's heart
believes in kindness and goodness. I hope
you become someone's savior.

If I, at any point, became the savior,
please remember me in your sincerest of
prayers. Maybe that's the best way you
can thank me and if you ever want

someone to listen to you, you can contact me anytime. I assure you that you won't go back with a heavy heart...

اس زندگی رواں میں بہت کھویا ، بہت پایا۔کہیں چپ رہ گئے کہیں بول پڑے یہ لب۔کہیں دُکھوں کا حساب نہ رہا کبھی خوشی کے بعد خوشی سے سامنا ہوا۔آج بہت عرصے بعد ماضی پر نظر پڑی تو لب مسکرا دیے کے شاید کچھ راستوں سے گزر کر ہی انسان فیصلہ کرسکتا ہے کہ اس نے کس راہ پر قدم رکھنے ہیں اور کونسی راہوں سے لا تعلق کردینا ہے خود کو

Thank you!

 Until next time! Till then stay happy and don't forget to be a kind person. We all need support and recovery. I hope this reached to you in time where you needed it the most.

Sincerely,
Samar Bakhtawar
Author of YOU
27th September, 2020.

.....and when someone comes around to
help you and make you understand
things , I hope you don't push them away
rather understand that they are exactly
who you need to grow and that they
keep the purest intentions for you. They
care for you and love you genuinely.

I hope you understand.